Things are made to happen."

Jack's Path

THE LIFE OF

WRITTEN BY **Doreen Rappaport**

# of Courage

John F. Kennedy

ILLUSTRATED BY **Matt Tavares**

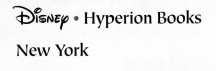 • Hyperion Books

New York

John F. Kennedy, called Jack
by family and friends,
was the second oldest
of four boys and five girls
in a wealthy, close-knit family.

Jack's mother read to her children every night;

"He always read more than any of the others."

Books took Jack on adventures with
the mischievous goat Billy Whisker,
with Peter Pan and Tinker Bell,
and with King Arthur's brave knights
in the kingdom of Camelot.

Jack's father pushed his children
to compete with each other
and do their very best:

"Come in a winner; second place is not good."

Jack's father's dream was
for his oldest son, Joe,
to become the first Catholic president
of the United States.

Joe excelled in everything.
Jack tried to keep up with Joe.
He didn't succeed in school, even
though his father pushed him to do better.

"I have been doing a little worrying about my studies because of what Dad said about me starting off great and then going down."

Joe was a college football star.
Jack tried out for the team, but
he wasn't strong enough
and hurt his back playing.
Swimming was his sport, and
he helped his team win many medals.

Jack's college record was only fair, but he received a better grade than Joe did on his senior thesis.

His father congratulated him:

"I always knew you were smart."

He sent Jack's thesis to a reporter who helped Jack rewrite it, gave it a more interesting title, and helped get it published.

Why England Slept made twenty-three-year-old Jack famous.

When Jack turned twenty-four,
the United States was at war.
Jack commanded a PT boat
in the South Pacific.
The Americans and Japanese
were locked in fierce combat.

"This job is really the great spot of the navy.
You are your own boss, and it's like sailing
around as in the old days."

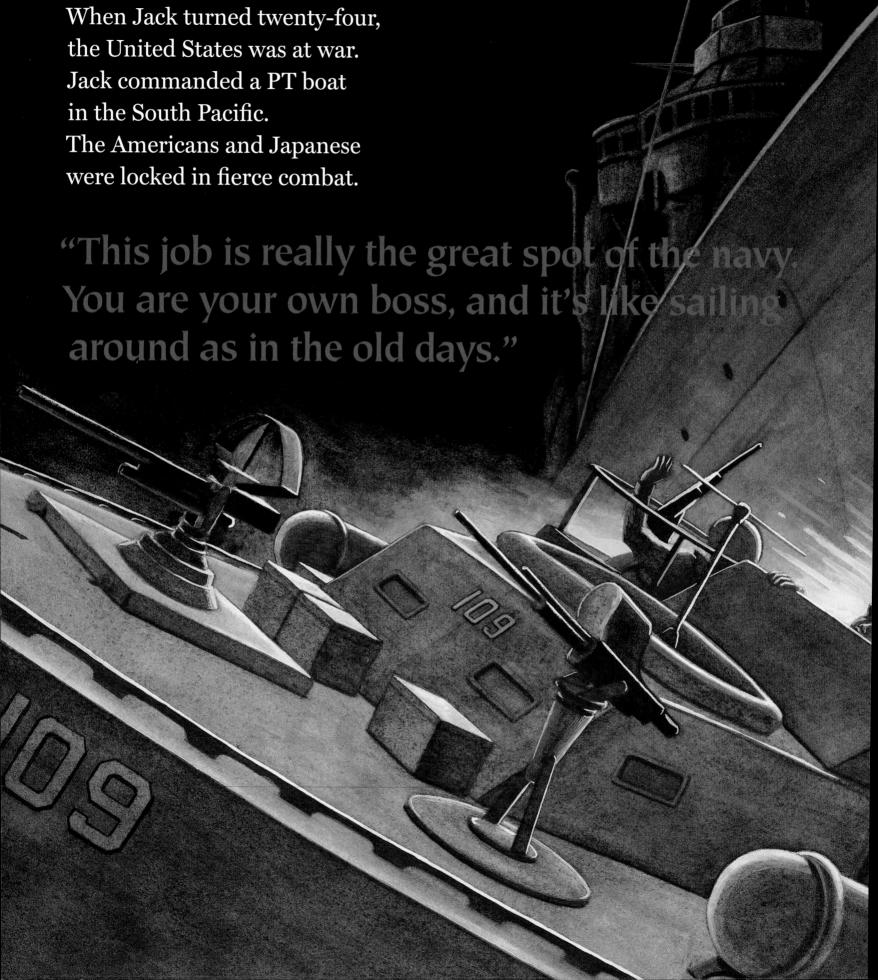

One night on a mission,
a Japanese destroyer rammed
Jack's PT boat, splitting it in half
and reinjuring Jack's back.
Two men died instantly.
The eleven survivors clung to the wreckage,
waiting to be rescued. No one came.
After nine hours, Jack ordered them to
swim.

One man was too burned to swim,
so Jack put the man's life-vest strap
between his teeth and pulled him.
After five hours, the crew reached
a small island four miles away.

Jack left his men there.

Currents battered his tired body
as he swam to an area
where PT boats patrolled.
He treaded water for an hour,
but no boats came.
He swam back to his men.

He battled the sea two more times
but did not find help.

After five days, two islanders
who were American scouts
found them.

Jack received three medals for
his courage and leadership.
Asked how he had become a hero,
he answered,

"It was involuntary. They sank my boat."

Joe was a courageous war pilot,
but on his fifty-first flight,
his plane exploded.
His death devastated the family.
Jack's father told Jack,
now that Joe was dead,
he had to go into politics.

"I can feel Pappy's eyes on the back of my neck."

Jack didn't think
he had the ability or the strength
to run for public office.
His back was never free from pain.

A year later, he ran for Congress
from a neighborhood in Boston.
For eight months, day and night,
he was at factories and shipyards,
on trolley cars and street corners,
and in barbershops and fire stations.
He shook thousands of hands and
gave hundreds of speeches.

He told women whose sons
had died in battle:

"My mother is a
Gold Star Mother, too."

People liked the handsome war hero,
with his warm smile, easy manner,
and seemingly endless energy.
He won the election easily.

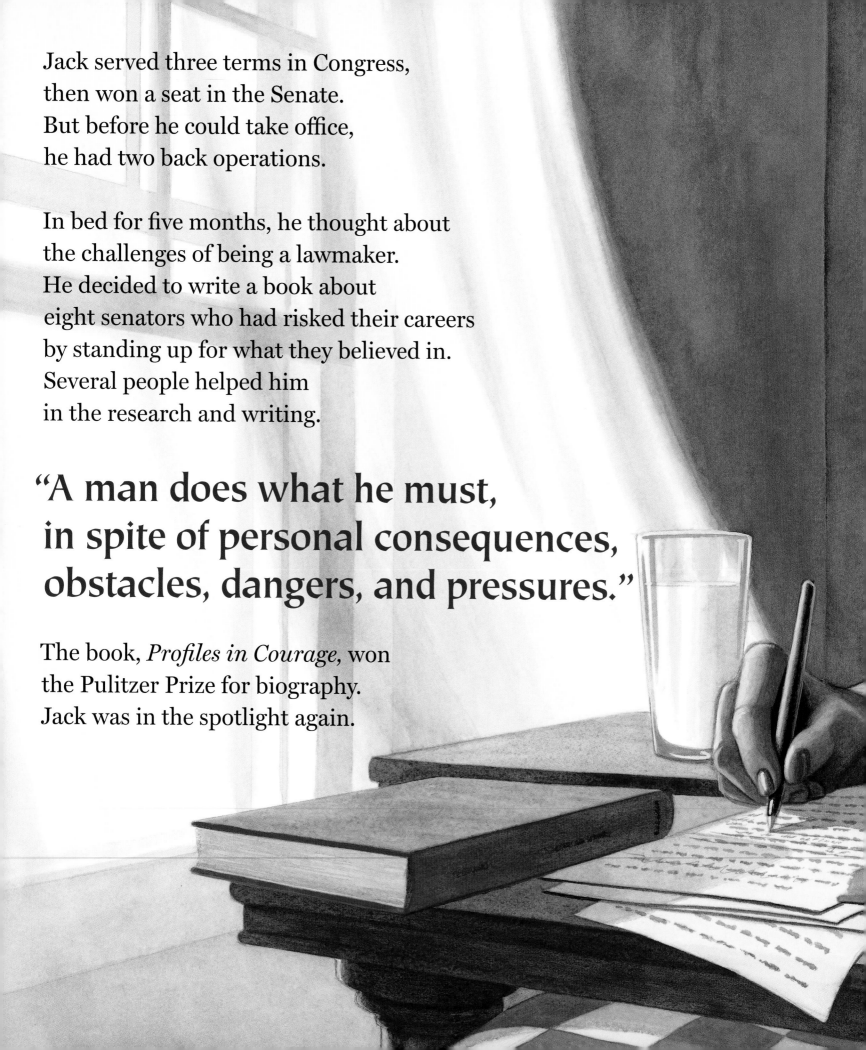

Jack served three terms in Congress,
then won a seat in the Senate.
But before he could take office,
he had two back operations.

In bed for five months, he thought about
the challenges of being a lawmaker.
He decided to write a book about
eight senators who had risked their careers
by standing up for what they believed in.
Several people helped him
in the research and writing.

"A man does what he must,
in spite of personal consequences,
obstacles, dangers, and pressures."

The book, *Profiles in Courage*, won
the Pulitzer Prize for biography.
Jack was in the spotlight again.

In 1960 he ran for president.
He created a message of hope and
used television to bring it to millions.

"We stand on the edge
of a new frontier.
The new frontier is not
a set of promises—
it is a set of challenges."

Americans liked his bold ideas.
But even friends said he could not win,
because he was Catholic.
Many people were prejudiced
against Catholics then.

Jack refused to ignore the issue.
He spoke directly about it on television.

"I believe in a president
whose views on religion
are his own private affair."

He narrowly won the election.

He asked his advisers to help
him make his inaugural speech
memorable and inspirational.
On a bitterly cold day, January 20, 1961,
the world listened to America's
youngest president ever elected:

"And so, my fellow Americans,
ask not what your country can do for you—
ask what you can do for your country.
My fellow citizens of the world:
ask not what America will do for you,
but what together we can do
for the freedom of man."

His words inspired people all over the globe.

The White House had a new spirit.
The elegant first lady,
Jacqueline Kennedy, welcomed
artists and writers and musicians
into her new home.
The Kennedy children,
John Jr. and Caroline, played
all over the White House grounds.

Americans enjoyed Kennedy's
directness and wit.

"How do you like being
president?"

"The problems are more difficult
than I thought they would be.
It is much easier to make
the speeches than
make the judgments."

Asked the question another time,
he playfully answered:

"The pay is good
and I can walk to work."

Few people knew that
the young vital president
had serious health problems
and was in constant pain.

The United States and the Soviet Union
competed for world power then.
The Soviets sent experts to help people
in developing countries.
Kennedy created the Peace Corps.

"We have men and women
anxious to sacrifice their energies
and time and toil to the
cause of world peace
and human progress."

Thousands of Americans,
young and old, built schools
and roads and sewers and
taught children all over the world.

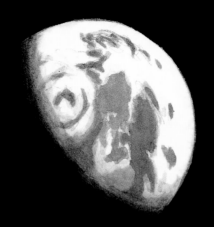

He announced that America
would beat the Soviets to the moon.

"We choose to go to the moon
in this decade,
and do the other things,
not because they are easy,
but because they are hard."

Less than ten years later,
two American astronauts
walked on the moon.

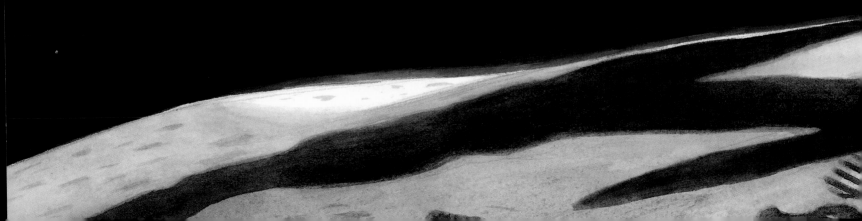

But not all of Kennedy's decisions were wise.

Three months into office,
he approved an invasion of Cuba,
a country ninety miles from Florida.
Cuba's leader was a Soviet ally.
The invasion was a disaster.

"I'm the responsible officer of the government,"

he told Americans on television.

Eight months later, the Soviets
put nuclear missiles, aimed at
the United States, in Cuba.
Kennedy demanded they be removed.
For thirteen anxious days,
the world feared war between
these two superpowers.
Finally the Soviets backed down,
and the United States pledged
not to invade Cuba.

The two superpowers had enough bombs
to destroy each other.
Kennedy wanted to end the weapons race.
His military advisers were against
any ban on testing weapons.

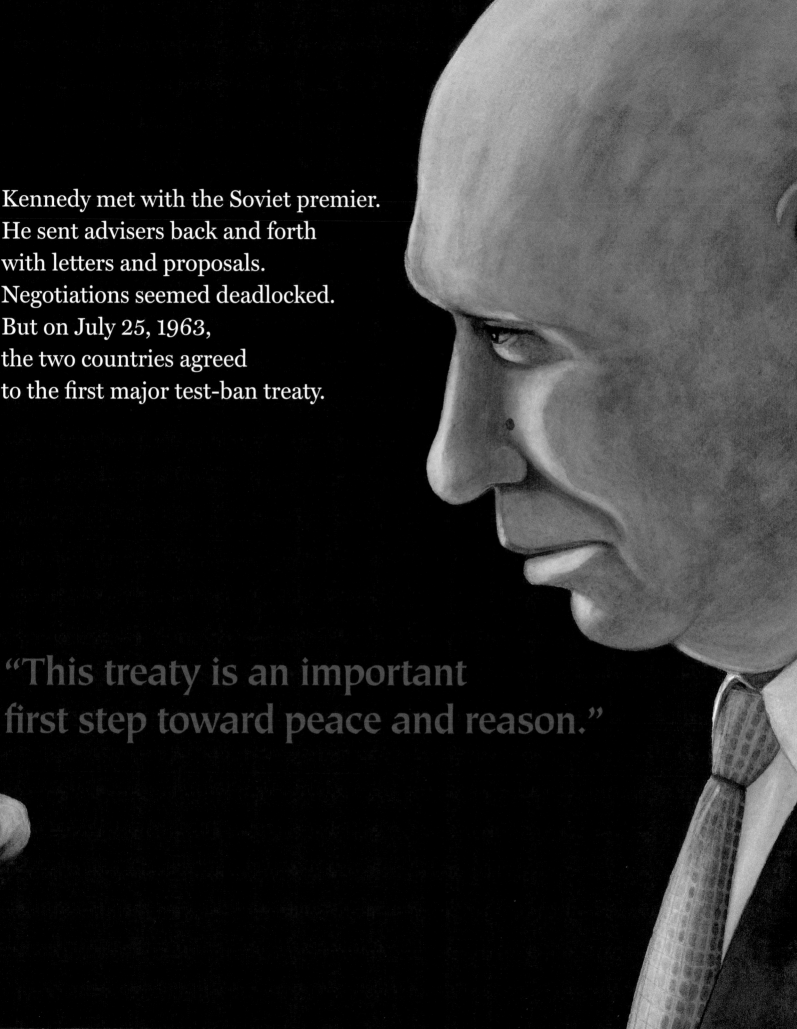

Kennedy met with the Soviet premier.
He sent advisers back and forth
with letters and proposals.
Negotiations seemed deadlocked.
But on July 25, 1963,
the two countries agreed
to the first major test-ban treaty.

"This treaty is an important
first step toward peace and reason."

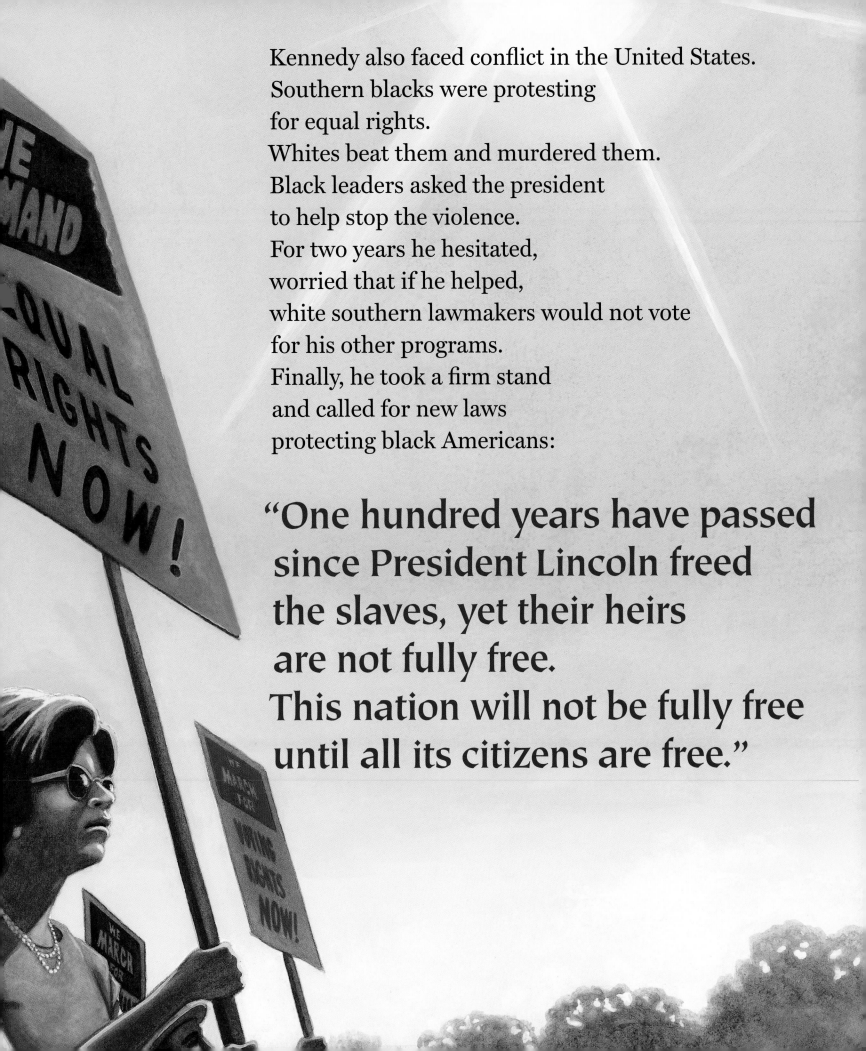

Kennedy also faced conflict in the United States.
Southern blacks were protesting
for equal rights.
Whites beat them and murdered them.
Black leaders asked the president
to help stop the violence.
For two years he hesitated,
worried that if he helped,
white southern lawmakers would not vote
for his other programs.
Finally, he took a firm stand
and called for new laws
protecting black Americans:

"One hundred years have passed
since President Lincoln freed
the slaves, yet their heirs
are not fully free.
This nation will not be fully free
until all its citizens are free."

In November 1963, Kennedy decided
to visit some western states where
he had done poorly with voters.
As thousands cheered his motorcade
through Dallas, Texas,
he was shot and killed.

His sudden death shocked
and saddened the world.

"A man may die,
nations may rise and fall,
but an idea lives on."

The new president, Lyndon B. Johnson,
carried out Kennedy's legacy.
Johnson used his political skills to
convince Congress to pass new programs
that bettered the lives of all Americans—
laws that guaranteed voting rights for all,
medical care for the elderly,
and educational opportunities for the very young.

Author's Note

The first national election I voted in was between John F. Kennedy and Richard M. Nixon in 1960. I remember grabbing the large envelope containing my absentee ballot out of the mailbox and running to show my roommates. It was a glorious moment, putting an X in the box next to Kennedy's name. His intelligence, youth, and vitality offered hope for the country.

His death overwhelmed everyone I knew. My friends and I clung together for three days, following every detail of his funeral on television. The procession was organized by Jacqueline Kennedy, herself only thirty-four years old then. A lasting image of that day, which still brings tears to my eyes, is three-year-old John Jr. (nicknamed John-John by the press) saluting his father's coffin.

John F. Kennedy has remained a symbol of hope and potential for the world

Illustrator's Note

I arrived at the audiovisual research room at the John F. Kennedy Presidential Library in Boston with a specific list of photographs I was hoping to find to use as visual references for my illustrations: pictures of JFK as a child, as a college student, as a young man campaigning for Congress, etc. The incredibly helpful archives specialist Laurie Austin took my list, disappeared into another room for a few minutes, then returned with several large file boxes, each one clearly labeled and filled with photographs.

I found most of what I was looking for, plus one treasure I did not expect: a box marked "Kennedy Family Photos." These were pictures taken by the Kennedys themselves. Most of them had nothing to do with the sketches I was working on, but there was something fascinating about them. There was one of Joe Jr. and Jack wrestling near the pool in Palm Beach, each holding the other in a headlock, Joe Jr. making a silly face for the camera. Another showed Bobby and Jean, probably six and four years old respectively, rowing a kid-size boat with the name "Bobby" painted on the side of it, while their older siblings goofed around in a bigger boat.

Growing up near Boston, I had always thought of the Kennedys as larger-than-life, like royalty. And in many ways, they were. But in these pictures they seemed so real, so human, so normal. I tried to keep this in mind as I illustrated this book, careful to show John F. Kennedy not only as an American icon, but also as a real human being.

Important Events

May 29, 1917: John Fitzgerald Kennedy is born to Rose and Joseph Kennedy.

October 1929: The stock market crash triggers the Great Depression.

Fall 1931–June 1935: JFK attends The Choate School in Connecticut.

Fall 1935: He leaves Princeton due to illness.

1936–1940: JFK attends Harvard University.

1937: His father becomes ambassador to Great Britain.

July 1940: JFK's senior thesis, *Why England Slept,* is published.

December 7, 1941: The Japanese bomb Pearl Harbor and the U. S. enters World War II.

1941–1945: Kennedy is a lieutenant in the United States Navy. On August 2, 1943, a Japanese
    destroyer splits his PT boat in half.

August 12, 1944: Joseph Kennedy Jr. is killed on his fifty-first flying mission.

January 3, 1947–January 1953: JFK represents Massachusetts's Eleventh District in the House of
    Representatives.

1950–1953: The United States is involved in the Korean War.

September 12, 1953: Jacqueline Bouvier and John F. Kennedy are married.

January 3, 1953–December 22, 1960: JFK serves as a U.S. senator from Massachusetts.

1956: Kennedy unsuccessfully seeks the Democratic Party vice-presidential nomination.

1957: Kennedy wins the Pulitzer Prize for *Profiles in Courage.*

November 27, 1957: Caroline Bouvier Kennedy is born.

November 4, 1958: JFK is elected to a second term in the Senate.

November 8, 1960: JFK is elected as the thirty-fifth president.

November 25, 1960: John Kennedy Jr. is born.

January 20, 1961: Kennedy is inaugurated as president.

March 1961: He announces the establishment of the Peace Corps.

April 1961: The invasion of Cuba fails.

June 1961: JFK and Nikita Khrushchev meet in Vienna, Austria.

August 1961: The Russians begin the construction of the Berlin Wall.

October 16–28, 1962: The Cuban missile crisis ends when Russia agrees to remove its missiles
    from Cuba.

June 16, 1963: Kennedy gives his "Ich bin ein Berliner" speech in German.

August 5, 1963: The United States and the Soviet Union agree to a limited nuclear test-ban treaty,
    which prohibits all tests of nuclear weapons, except underground.

November 22, 1963: JFK is assassinated in Dallas, Texas. Lyndon Johnson becomes president.

Selected Research Sources

Dallek, Robert. *An Unfinished Life: John F. Kennedy, 1917–1963*. Boston: Little, Brown and Company, 2003.

Kennedy, John F. *As We Remember Joe*. Cambridge, Mass.: Privately published, 1945.

———, ed. *A Nation of Immigrants*. Rev. and enlarged ed., with introduction by Robert F. Kennedy and new preface by John P. Roche. New York: Harper & Row, 1986.

———. *Profiles in Courage*. Memorial ed. New York: Harper & Row, 1964.

———. *Why England Slept*. Reprint. Westport, Conn.: Greenwood Press, 1981.

Manchester, William. *Remembering Kennedy: One Brief Shining Moment*. Boston: Little, Brown and Company, 1983.

Nevins, Allan, ed. *The Strategy of Peace*. New York: Harper & Row, 1960.

O'Donnell, Kenneth P. and David F. Powers. *"Johnny, We Hardly Knew Ye": Memories of John Fitzgerald Kennedy*. Boston: Little, Brown and Company, 1972.

Parmet, Herbert S. *Jack: The Struggles of John F. Kennedy*. New York: Dial Press, 1980.

———. *JFK: The Presidency of John F. Kennedy*. New York: Dial Press, 1983.

Sorensen, Theodore C., comp. *"Let the Word Go Forth": The Speeches, Statements, and Writings of John F. Kennedy*. New York: Dell Publishing, 1991.

White, Theodore H. *The Making of the President, 1960*. Reprint. New York: Atheneum, 1988.

Web site: John F. Kennedy Presidential Library and Museum. www.jfklibrary.org

If you want to learn more about John F. Kennedy, you can read

Adler, David. *A Picture Book of John F. Kennedy*. Illustrated by Robert F. Casilla. New York: Holiday House, 1991.

Cooper, Ilene. *Jack: The Early Years of John F. Kennedy*. New York: Dutton, 2003.

Frisbee, Lucy Frost. *John Fitzgerald Kennedy: America's Youngest President*. Illustrated by Al Fiorentino. New York: Simon & Schuster, 1986.

Heiligman, Deborah. *High Hopes: A Photobiography of John F. Kennedy*. Washington, D.C.: National Geographic, 2003.

Kaplan, Howard S. *John F. Kennedy: A Photographic Story of a Life*. New York: Dorling Kindersley Publishing, 2004.

McDonough, Yona Zeldis. *Who Was John F. Kennedy?* Illustrated by Nancy Harrison and Jill Weber. New York: Penguin, 2005.

O'Brien, Michael. *John F. Kennedy: A Biography*. New York: St. Martin's Press, 2005.

For Jared Rosegarten, with hugs and love
—D. R.

In memory of Christopher Behney Moore
—M. T.

———————⬤———————

ACKNOWLEDGMENTS: I thank Annmarie McLeoud and the students in Sirlenda Maxwell's
fifth grade class at CS 21, Brooklyn, New York, for their insightful and truthful critiques of my book.
I thank Herbert B. Parmet, Professor Emeritus, Graduate Center, CUNY, New York, for sharing his vast knowledge.
Laurie Austin and Mayrose Grossman in the audiovisual archives of the
John F. Kennedy Presidential Library provided essential assistance.

In many instances, quotes by President Kennedy have been shortened without changing their meaning.
Punctuation has been simpified. The Kennedy quotes come from personal letters and
comments to friends (pages 5–12, 15–16), press conferences (13–14, 25–26),
and speeches (2–3, 17–18, 21–24, 27–40) and his book *Profiles In Courage* (46–47).

Hand lettering by John Stevens
This book is set in 18-point Miller Text.

First Edition
10 9 8 7 6 5 4 3 2 1
F850-6835-5-10196
Printed in Singapore
Reinforced binding

Library of Congress Cataloging-in-Publication Data on file.
ISBN 978-1-4231-2272-2
Visit www.hyperionbooksforchildren.com

"The stories of past courage can teach,
they can offer hope,
they can provide inspiration.